"Kiss The Son"

Bertron James Hamill

HAMILL

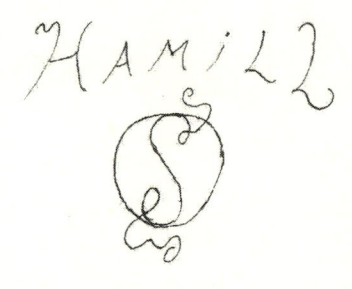

Be it word or thought
I pray that they are profitable
And not having my own "vain thoughts"

These are the works of

Bertron

of the

Scarred One

"All scriptures... is profitable..."
2 Tim. 3:16

Contents:

5 – (introduction) In Reckoning of Words

6 – Psalm 2

7 – Man

10 – Sin

21 – The Son

15 – Promises of Faith In Christ

17 - Appendix

18 - Death

19 – The Bridge

23 – Psalm 2 (cross-references)

28 – What is the Gospel?

"But not as the offence, so also is the free gift. For if through the offence of one many be dead, much more the grace of God, and the gift by grace, which is by one man, Jesus Christ, hath abounded unto many. ... Therefore as by the offence of one judgment came upon all men to condemnation; even so by the righteousness of one the free gift came upon all men unto justification of life." Rom.5:15, 18

"Kiss the Son, lest he be angry, and ye perish from the way, when his wrath is kindled but a little. Blessed are all they that put their trust in him." Ps.2:12

"For God so loved the world, that he gave his only begotten Son, that whosoever believeth in him should not perish, but have everlasting life. For God sent not his Son into the world to condemn the world; but that the world through him might be saved. He that believeth on him is not condemned: but he that believeth not is condemned already, because he hath not believed in the name of the only begotten Son of God." Jn.3:16-18

"He that believeth on the Son hath everlasting life: and he that believeth not the Son shall not see life; but the wrath of God abideth on him." Jn.3:36

In Reckoning of Words

These works are but words of 'teaching and admonishing' concerning some 'things' that I have seen, and in understanding according to the guidance of the 'Spirit of Truth', which is the Holy Spirit or the Comforter, through the Word (John14:26; 16:13; 17:17).

Be it known to take note that I am but a man, and my words are not the 'Truths' of the Word (John17:17). And never is it intended that my words should be treated as such. For the 'right kind of faith' comes from one place alone, the Word (Rom.10:17). Far be it that any man should believe by my words. Why should his faith be placed in me, instead of Christ where it should be (1Cor.1:17; 2:1, 4-5)? Is it not His word that is 'like a fire and a hammer that breaketh the rock in pieces', and is it not 'quick and powerful and sharper than any two-edged sword' (Jer.23:29, Heb.4:12). Alas, does it not speak of the Bereans in Acts17:10-11, that how they received the gospel, and yet did not believe in Paul and Silas, but went to the scriptures to determine by faith in the Word. Wherefore, I have indexed each work both as citing the references and the scriptures themselves which are the 'origination' of these works of thoughts, that all readers may be as the Bereans. For if by encouragement and admonishing of these works, any man is stimulated to look to the scriptures so that he receives understanding from the Spirit through the Word, which does not return void (Is.55:11), and moves (acts) according to the thing which is understood, then the purpose of these works is fulfilled. May the Lord be glorified.

"Whether, therefore, ye eat, or drink, or whatever ye do, do all to the glory of God."

1Cor.10:31

Psalm 2

1 "Why do the heathen rage, and the people imagine a vain thing?"

2 "The kings of the earth set themselves, and the rulers take counsel together, against the LORD, and against his anointed, saying,"

3 "Let us break their bands asunder, and cast away their cords from us."

4 "He that sitteth in the heavens shall laugh: the Lord shall have them in derision."

5 "Then shall he speak unto them in his wrath, and vex them in his sore displeasure."

6 "Yet have I set my king upon my holy hill of Zion."

7 "I will declare the decree: the LORD hath said unto me, Thou art my Son; this day have I begotten thee."

8 "Ask of me, and I shall give thee the heathen for thine inheritance, and the uttermost parts of the earth for thy possession."

9 "Thou shalt break them with a rod of iron; thou shalt dash them in pieces like a potter's vessel."

10 "Be wise now therefore, O ye kings: be instructed, ye judges of the earth."

11 " Serve the LORD with fear, and rejoice with trembling."

12 "Kiss the Son, lest he be angry, and ye perish from the way, when his wrath is kindled but a little. Blessed are all they that put their trust in him."

Man

~ Bertron J. Hamill

"... and man became a living soul."

Gen.2:7

"In the beginning God created the heaven and the earth."

Later, he created man from the dirt

Made in God's *image*

A soul that was *living*

Unto whom a commandment was given

A fruit, not to be eaten

In which commandment, he said a promise

In the day, when eaten

Life, he would lose it

But when he ate, his eyes opened

Because of that fruit of knowing

But did he die?

Or did God lie?

At 'Nine hundred and thirty' did Adam die

That is to say, physically

But is there any other kind of death, really?

Here is the question

That by Adam, "...death passed upon all men..."?

Do "all men" die physically?

But accordingly, believers will be resurrected, flying

So, what is "all men"?

But that we, believers, Were *DEAD IN SINS*

So, death came to that soul that was living

Alas! The damage

That Adam's son and generations are begotten,

Not in God's, but in Adam's image

Thus, became the nature of man in whole

Death to Adam's living soul

Just in one simple way

It happened, that day

~

Index:

Gen. 1:1 "In the beginning God created the heaven and the earth."

Gen. 1:27 "So God created man in his own image, in the image of God created he him; male and female created he them."

Gen. 2:7 "And the LORD God formed man of the dust of the ground, and breathed into his nostrils the breath of life; and man became a living soul."

Gen. 2:17 "But of the tree of the knowledge of good and evil, thou shalt not eat of it: for in the day that thou eatest thereof thou shalt surely die."

Gen. 3:6 "And when the woman saw that the tree was good for food, and that it was pleasant to the eyes, and a tree to be desired to make one wise, she took of the fruit thereof, and did eat, and gave also unto her husband with her; and he did eat."

Gen. 3:7 "And the eyes of them both were opened, and they knew that they were naked; and they sewed fig leaves together, and made themselves aprons."

Gen. 5:5 "And all the days that Adam lived were nine hundred and thirty years: and he died."

Rom. 5:12 "Wherefore, as by one man sin entered into the world, and death by sin; and so death passed upon all men, for that all have sinned:"

1Th. 4:16 "For the Lord himself shall descend from heaven with a shout, with the voice of the archangel, and with the trump of God: and the dead in Christ shall rise first:"

1Th. 4:17 "Then we which are alive and remain shall be caught up together with them in the clouds, to meet the Lord in the air: and so shall we ever be with the Lord."

Eph. 2:5 "Even when we were dead in sins, hath quickened us together with Christ, (by grace ye are saved;)" ['Even when WE' => Eph.1:1 – believers]

Gen. 5:3 "And Adam lived an hundred and thirty years, and begat a son in his own likeness, after his image; and called his name Seth:"

Sin

~ Bertron J. Hamill

"For all have sinned, and come short of the glory of God,"

Rom.3:23

Adam disobeyed and sinned

And by sin, man and God are far separated from end to end

And sin is upon all men

By which they fall short

And deaths there are more

Because of sin, another death

An eternal fiery death

Can a man that is dead in sin, do anything?

In the grave, there is no work, nor device, nor anything

'For we are saved by grace

Through faith'

'Not by works, lest we should boast'

How simple is this?

Grace is not of works

And works is not of grace

For our works is our own righteousness

Our own is like filth

And away our iniquities have taken us

~

Index:

Isa. 59:1 "Behold, the LORD'S hand is not shortened, that it cannot save; neither his ear heavy, that it cannot hear:"

Isa. 59:2 "But your iniquities have separated between you and your God, and your sins have hid his face from you, that he will not hear."

Rom. 3:23 " For all have sinned, and come short of the glory of God;"

Rom. 6:23 "For the wages of sin is death; but the gift of God is eternal life through Jesus Christ our Lord."

Rev. 20:14 "And death and hell were cast into the lake of fire. This is the second death."

Rev. 20:15 "And whosoever was not found written in the book of life was cast into the lake of fire."

Ecc. 9:10b "...for there is no work, nor device, nor knowledge, nor wisdom, in the grave, whither thou goest."

Eph. 2:8 "For by grace are ye saved through faith; and that not of yourselves: it is the gift of God:"

Eph. 2:9 "Not of works, lest any man should boast."

Rom. 11:6 "And if by grace, then is it no more of works: otherwise grace is no more grace. But if it be of works, then is it no more grace: otherwise work is no more work."

Tit. 3:5 "Not by works of righteousness which we have done, but according to his mercy he saved us, by the washing of regeneration, and renewing of the Holy Ghost;"

Isa. 64:6 "But we are all as an unclean thing, and all our righteousnesses are as filthy rags; and we all do fade as a leaf; and our iniquities, like the wind, have taken us away."

Rom. 4:4 "Now to him that worketh is the reward not reckoned of grace, but of debt."

Rom. 4:5 "But to him that worketh not, but believeth on him that justifieth the ungodly, his faith is counted for righteousness."

The Son

~ Bertron J. Hamill

"And I saw, and bore witness that this is the Son of God"

Jn.1:34

~

The Son, God hath called God

The Son, the king: "Therefore God, thy God"

He was from the beginning

He had the Father's glory

He is the Word made flesh

And Jesus, is the Son, in context

Even in the book of John

Which was written, that we might believe that he is the Son

What is Christ? What does it mean?

Today, men claim to be wise

"Oh, it's his last name", said they

But as in Acts it mentions Christ

It quotes a passage in Psalm 2, that calls it otherwise

'The Anointed'

What is Messiah? What do men say?

But the Hebrew word of Messiah, is also the same word, for 'the anointed'

The Son was given

He died, was buried, and is risen

Our trespasses were nailed to the cross, and forgiven

For our sins, He is the propitiation

He is the way, none can come to the Father, but through Him

~

Index:

Heb. 1:8 "But unto the Son he saith, Thy throne, O God, is for ever and ever: a sceptre of righteousness is the sceptre of thy kingdom."

Heb. 1:9 "Thou hast loved righteousness, and hated iniquity; therefore God, even thy God, hath anointed thee with the oil of gladness above thy fellows."

Psa. 45:1 "To the chief Musician upon Shoshannim, for the sons of Korah, Maschil, A Song of loves. My heart is inditing a good matter: I speak of the things which I have made touching the king: my tongue is the pen of a ready writer."

Psa. 45:2 "Thou art fairer than the children of men: grace is poured into thy lips: therefore God hath blessed thee for ever."

Psa. 45:6 "Thy throne, O God, is for ever and ever: the sceptre of thy kingdom is a right sceptre."

Psa. 45:7 "Thou lovest righteousness, and hatest wickedness: therefore God, thy God, hath anointed thee with the oil of gladness above thy fellows."

Joh. 1:1 "In the beginning was the Word, and the Word was with God, and the Word was God."

Joh. 1:14 "And the Word was made flesh, and dwelt among us, (and we beheld his glory, the glory as of the only begotten of the Father,) full of grace and truth."

Joh. 1:29 "The next day John seeth Jesus coming unto him, and saith, Behold the Lamb of God, which taketh away the sin of the world."

Joh. 1:34 "And I saw, and bare record that this is the Son of God."

Joh. 20:30 "And many other signs truly did Jesus in the presence of his disciples, which are not written in this book:"

Joh. 20:31 "But these are written, that ye might believe that Jesus is the Christ, the Son of God; and that believing ye might have life through his name."

Act. 4:25 "Who by the mouth of thy servant David hast said, Why did the heathen rage, and the people imagine vain things?"

Act. 4:26 "The kings of the earth stood up, and the rulers were gathered together against the Lord, and against his Christ."

Psa. 2:1 "Why do the heathen rage, and the people imagine a vain thing?"

Psa. 2:2 "The kings of the earth set themselves, and the rulers take counsel together, against the LORD, and against his anointed, saying,"

Dan. 9:24 "Seventy weeks are determined upon thy people and upon thy holy city, to finish the transgression, and to make an end of sins, and to make reconciliation for iniquity, and to bring in everlasting righteousness, and to seal up the vision and prophecy, and to anoint the most Holy."

Dan. 9:25 "Know therefore and understand, that from the going forth of the commandment to restore and to build Jerusalem unto the Messiah the Prince shall be seven weeks, and threescore and two weeks: the street shall be built again, and the wall, even in troublous times."

Joh. 3:16 "For God so loved the world, that he gave his only begotten Son, that whosoever believeth in him should not perish, but have everlasting life."

1Co. 15:3 "For I delivered unto you first of all that which I also received, how that Christ died for our sins according to the scriptures;"

1Co. 15:4 "And that he was buried, and that he rose again the third day according to the scriptures:"

Col. 2:13 "And you, being dead in your sins and the uncircumcision of your flesh, hath he quickened together with him, having forgiven you all trespasses;"

Col. 2:14 "Blotting out the handwriting of ordinances that was against us, which was contrary to us, and took it out of the way, nailing it to his cross;"

1Jn. 2:1 "My little children, these things write I unto you, that ye sin not. And if any man sin, we have an advocate with the Father, Jesus Christ the righteous:"

1Jn. 2:2 "And he is the propitiation for our sins: and not for ours only, but also for the sins of the whole world."

Joh. 14:6 "Jesus saith unto him, I am the way, the truth, and the life: no man cometh unto the Father, but by me."

Promises of Faith In Christ

~ Bertron J. Hamill

"...he is faithful that promised..."

Heb.10:23

~

So much in Christ by faith

So much did he promise

That eternal life, and passed from death

We have God's righteousness

Sealed with the Holy Spirit, are those who believed

Believe, and are saved

On his name, we have faith, and are born again

Born of God, and not of the will of men

Alas, to believe that Christ raised again

Is a prayer required? Or simply is the heart convinced?

"For with the heart man believes unto righteousness"

~

Index:

Joh. 5:24 "Verily, verily, I say unto you, He that heareth my word, and believeth on him that sent me, hath everlasting life, and shall not come into condemnation; but is passed from death unto life."

Rom. 3:22 "Even the righteousness of God which is by faith of Jesus Christ unto all and upon all them that believe: for there is no difference:"

Eph. 1:13 "In whom ye also trusted, after that ye heard the word of truth, the gospel of your salvation: in whom also after that ye believed, ye were sealed with that holy Spirit of promise,"

Act. 16:31 "And they said, Believe on the Lord Jesus Christ, and thou shalt be saved, and thy house."

Act. 16:34 "And when he had brought them into his house, he set meat before them, and rejoiced, believing in God with all his house."

Joh. 3:3 "Jesus answered and said unto him, Verily, verily, I say unto thee, Except a man be born again, he cannot see the kingdom of God."

Joh. 1:12 "But as many as received him, to them gave he power to become the sons of God, even to them that believe on his name:"

Joh. 1:13 "Which were born, not of blood, nor of the will of the flesh, nor of the will of man, but of God."

Rom. 10:9 "That if thou shalt confess with thy mouth the Lord Jesus, and shalt believe in thine heart that God hath raised him from the dead, thou shalt be saved."

Rom. 10:10 "For with the heart man believeth unto righteousness; and with the mouth confession is made unto salvation."

Appendix:

Death

Rom.5:12-19

Rom.6:23

Rev.20:14-15

    1) Dead in Sin =   Eph.2:5, Col.2:13 – dead in sin
                               Gen.2:7- man a living soul
                               Gen.2:17- the promise of death within the same day
                               Gen.3:7- the effects and acknowledgment of the spiritual death
                               Gen.5:3- born in man's image, (Gen.1:27)

    2) Physical Death = Heb.9:27

    3) 2nd. Death = Rev.20:14-15

2Cor. 5:14 – all men were dead

1Thess. 4:16 – 17 – not all men die of the Physical Death

Rev.20:14-15 – not all men die the 2nd. Death

Adam

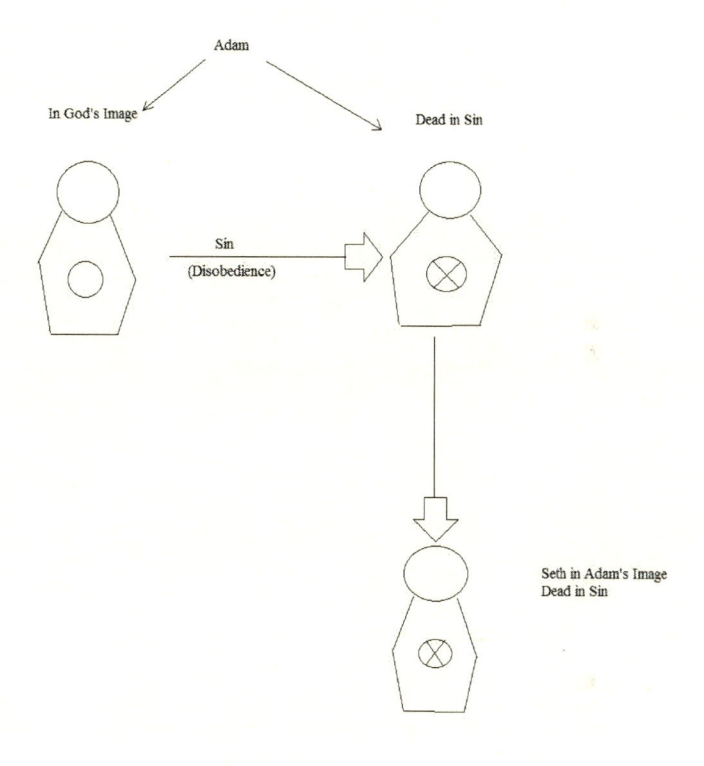

In God's Image — Dead in Sin

Sin
(Disobedience)

Seth in Adam's Image
Dead in Sin

The Bridge

Who was the first man?

Gen.2:21 – Adam

Gen.1:27 – God created man. What God? => Gen.1:1 – the God who created everything.

Gen.1:27 – in God's image => Gen.2:7 – ...and man became a "living" *soul*.

So Adam's soul was in God's image.

But God said in Gen.2:17. => the promise of death

Gen.3:7 – after he ate

Gen.5:3 – Adam's son was born in Adam's image not God's

So, did he die?

Rom.5:12 – sin entered the world, and death by sin

1Thes..4:16-17 – not all men die the physical death

Eph.2:5 – We were dead in sins

Adam (in God's image) => Adam: after he ate, sin entered the world (his soul died)
↓
Adam's son: Seth (born in Adam's image, not God's)

So Adam's soul died that day.

So, Adam's soul died in sin, and his son, Seth's soul was dead in sin. Rom.5:12. So, who all has sin?

Rom.3:23 – all sin

So, we all sin. What else happened?

Is.59:1-2 – Man was separated from God by Sin.

Since we are dead in sin, and are separated from God by sin, what will happen to us?

Rom.6:23 – the penalty of sin is Death

We're already dead in sin, we're already dying the physical death. What death is this talking about?

Well, it talks about the gift being eternal life, so apparently it is talking about an eternal death. What eternal death?

Rev.20:14-15 – the lake of fire – the 2nd. Death

It's obvious that this is the penalty of sin.

Who wants to go there?

Some might think… Surely, it isn't going to get fixed without us doing something good. Well, they mean that since a bad work broke it, surely, a good work will fix it.

Rom.4:3a - 'What saith the scripture…'

Eph.2:8-9 – it is by grace, by faith, not of ourselves, a gift (you never bought your own gift did you, I mean it was freely given, you didn't earn it), Not by Works lest we should boast.

Rom. 11:6 – grace is not of works, and works is not of grace

So, good deeds, prayer, and water baptism isn't going to bring our dead soul to life.

Some have a hard time with this; wherefore, here is a little more to confirm.

Tit.3:5 – not by works of Our righteousness

Is.64:6 – Our righteousness is as filthy rags

Rom.4:4-5 – our works is the reward not of grace but of debt

Here, some might say that it doesn't matter then, that we are in sin anyway and we can't do anything, so it doesn't matter if we just go on sinning whatever we want then does it?

Well, we have a purpose.

Ecc.12:13 – man's duty: fear God and keep his commandments

Is.43:7 – created for his glory, to glorify him.

Only problem is, we can't do that when we're dead in sin. – Ecc.9:10b

Then, God gave his Son.

John3:16 – His only begotten Son

1Cor.15:3-4

- So, Christ came, died for our sins, was buried, and rose again the third day according to scriptures.

John14:6 – And, Christ is the only way, The Way, There is nothing else.

Through faith in Christ we:

John 5:24, John20:31 – have Eternal Life

Rom.3:22 – are righteous, that is, having God's righteousness

Eph.1:12-13 – are sealed with the Holy Spirit

Acts16:31 – are saved

    Does that mean our whole house too? Well! Read on through verse thirty-four.

    Only those of ourr house that believes.

John 3:3, John1:12-13 – are Born Again.

So, what must we do?

Rom.10:9-10

So, does that mean that if I say with my oral mouth that God raised Jesus from the dead, I will be saved?

Can it be just from the oral mouth?

Read verse ten.

It says that 'with the heart man believes unto righteousness', be careful not to put faith in prayer being that it's only a work. – Eph.2:8-9.

Rom.5:12-19 - summary

Rom. 5:12-19

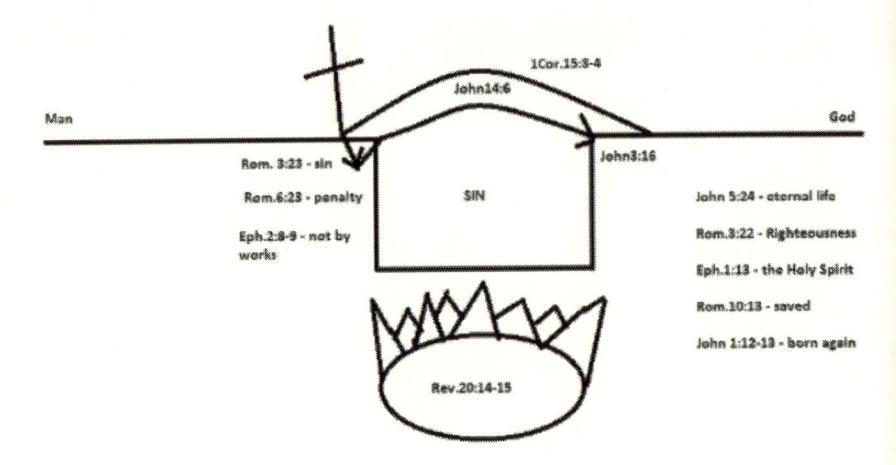

1Cor.15:3-4
John14:6

Man God

Rom. 3:23 - sin John3:16
Rom.6:23 - penalty SIN John 5:24 - eternal life
Eph.2:8-9 - not by works Rom.3:22 - Righteousness
 Eph.1:13 - the Holy Spirit
 Rom.10:13 - saved
 John 1:12-13 - born again

Rev.20:14-15

Psalm 2

Cross References:

Vs.1

"vain thing"

Deut.32:46-47 – the word is not a vain thing

Ps.119:113 – I hate vain thoughts, but thy law do I love

Is.55:8-9 – Our thoughts are not His thoughts, nor our ways His ways.

"imagine"

Hos.7

:1 – context is talking about the iniquity of Ephraim

:15 – they "imagine" 'mischief against him'

Next chapter:

Hos.8

:11 – context is talking about Ephraim

:12

    - the word written to him

      - he counted it as a strange thing.

Vs.2

"kings of the earth"

Ps.76

:12 – He is fearsome/terrible to the kings of the earth

:7 – Thou art to be feared

Deut.17:19 – learn to fear the Lord

"against the Lord"

1Sam.26:23 – David and Saul – David would not stretch his hand against the Lord's anointed.

Prov.21:30 – "There is no wisdom, nor understanding, nor counsel against the Lord."

Vs.3

"bands"

Hos.1:1 – The word of the Lord = The Lord speaking

11:4 – bands of love

1Jn.4:10 – love = God loved us in that he sent His Son to be the propitiation.

1Jn.2:22 – denying the Father and the Son   =   "against the Lord and His Anointed"

Vs.4

"sitteth on the heavens"

Is.40:22 – The Almighty that they're dealing with!!!

"laugh"

Ps.59:5-8 – shall laugh at them, and shall have all of the nations in derision

Vs.5

"wrath"

Eph.2

:1-2 – we were children of disobedience →   Col.3:6 – the wrath of God came upon the children of disobedience

:3 – we were children of wrath

:4   Rom.5:8-10

    - God is rich in mercy   - saved from wrath through him

    - with great love he hath loved   - even when we were enemies hath

:5   reconciled us

    - we were dead in sin

    - are made alive with Christ

1Thess.1:10 – Jesus hath delivered us from the "wrath" to come

Jn.3:36

    - believe on the Son → everlasting lif

    - believe not on the Son → then the "wrath" of God abides

Vs.6

Ps.89:18 – The Holy One is the King

Ps.45

:1-2 – talking to the king

:6-7 – The King is God

Heb.1:8 – the King is the Son

Vs.7

Heb.1:5

- quoting 2Sam.7:12-14a – "I will be his father, and he shall be my son."

- "Today have I begotten thee."

Heb.5:5 – The Father glorified the Son to be made an high priest

Acts13:33 – "Today have I begotten thee" = Christ raised from the dead

- Eph.1:19-20

:19 – worked to us-ward

:20 – raised from the dead and set at the right hand of God

Vs.8

Ps8:3-6 – Heb.2:7,9 – Ps.8 is talking about Christ

Ps.8:3-6 – Christ to inherit all things

Vs.9

"rod of iron"

Rev.2

:26 – given Him power over the nations

:27 – rule them with a rod of iron

Rev.19:15

- smite the nations

- rule them with a rod of iron

Vs.10

2Tim.3:16 – All Scriptures… is profitable… for instruction

Prov.8

:1-4 – the context is that this is wisdom speaking

:32 – hearken unto wisdom, keep its ways

:33 – hear instruction, be wise, do not refuse it

Prov.19

:20 – Hear counsel, receive instruction that ye may be wise

:21 – the counsel of the Lord, it shall stand

Ps.111:10 – The fear of the Lord is the beginning of wisdom

Vs.11

2Chron.30:8 – serve the Lord that his wrath may turn away

Ps.111:10 – The fear of the Lord is the beginning of wisdom, good understanding have all they that do/keep his commandments.

Vs.12

Jn.3:14-18 = Jn.3:36 – believe – shall not perish, have everlasting life; believe not – perish, wrath of God abides

Rom.5:8-9 – saved from wrath through him

Jn.5

:22 – judgment committed unto the Son

:23 – He that honoreth not the Son, honoreth not the Father

:24 – believe – have everlasting life, shall not come into judgment/condemnation, is passed from death unto life.

What is the Gospel?

2Tim.1:8

    - Jesus was of the seed of David => He was human

    - was raised from the dead

Acts15:7 =>Acts10:34-43

Acts10:34-43

    - He is Lord of all => He is God

    - He is anointed with the Holy Spirit

    - was slain and hanged on tree => He died for us

    - God raised him up the third day => He rose from the dead

    - He is ordained to judge the living and the dead => through Him we are judged

    - Whoever believes on Him shall receive remission of sins

Rom.1:15-16

    - power of God unto salvation to everyone that believes => Saved

1Cor.15:3-4

    - Saved

    - died for our sins

Eph.1:13

    - Sealed with the Holy Spirit

2Tim.1:8-10

    - saved us

    - called us

    - not by works

    - by grace

    - brought life => Eternal Life

Rom.2:16

    - God judging the secrets of men by Jesus Christ => Judged through Him

Acts20:24

    - by grace

1Tim.1:8-11

    - the law says we're guilty

Rom.3:19-20

    - the law says we're guilty

Gal.3:8

    - the gospel preached unto Abraham

    - "In thee shall all the nations of the earth be blessed."

=> Gen.12:3

    - "In thee shall all families of the earth be blessed."

=> Acts 3:25

    - "And in thy seed shall all the kindreds of the earth be blessed."

=> Gal.3:16

    - in his seed (singular) [Christ], not seeds (plural)

=> Gal.3:6-7

    - In Christ made righteous by faith

    - receive the Holy Spirit through faith

Listed:

~This is the content of the gospel~

a) He is human

b) He is God

c) He is anointed with the Holy Spirit

d) He died for us

e) He rose from the dead

f) Through Him, all are judged

g) Saved

h) Remission of sins

i) Sealed with the Holy Spirit

j) Not by works

k) By grace

l) Eternal life

m) The law tells us we're guilty

n) In Christ, we are made righteous by faith

"For the Father judgeth no man, but hath committed all judgment unto the Son: That all men should honour the Son, even as they honour the Father. He that honoureth not the Son honoureth not the Father which hath sent him. Verily, verily, I say unto you, He that heareth my word, and believeth on him that sent me, hath everlasting life, and shall not come into condemnation; but is passed from death unto life. Verily, verily, I say unto you, The hour is coming, and now is, when the dead shall hear the voice of the Son of God: and they that hear shall live. For as the Father hath life in himself; so hath he given to the Son to have life in himself; And hath given him authority to execute judgment also, because he is the Son of man." Jn. 5:22-27

Made in the USA
Columbia, SC
23 December 2023